Just Enough
Difficult Topics Made Easy

Where Do Babies Come From?

Our First Talk About Birth

Dr. Jillian Roberts

illustrated by

Cindy Revell

ORCA BOOK PUBLISHERS

Published in Canada and the United States in 2022 by Orca Book Publishers.
Previously published in 2015 by Orca Book Publishers as a
hardcover (ISBN 9781459809420) and available as an ebook
(ISBN 9781459809437, PDF; ISBN 9781459809444, EPUB).
orcabook.com

Library and Archives Canada Cataloguing in Publication
Title: Where do babies come from? : our first talk about birth
/ Dr. Jillian Roberts ; illustrated by Cindy Revell.
Names: Roberts, Jillian, 1971- author. | Revell, Cindy, illustrator.
Series: Roberts, Jillian, 1971- Just enough.
Description: Series statement: Just enough: difficult
topics made easy | Previously published: 2015.
Identifiers: Canadiana 20210169303 | ISBN 9781459831865 (softcover)
Subjects: LCSH: Human reproduction—Juvenile literature. |
LCSH: Childbirth—Juvenile literature. | LCSH: Sex instruction for children.
Classification: LCC QP251.5 .R63 2022 | DDC j612.6—dc23

Library of Congress Control Number: 2021934734

Summary: A nonfiction picture book that introduces
very young children to the basics of reproduction in a
way that is gentle, age-appropriate and accessible.

Orca Book Publishers is committed to reducing the consumption
of nonrenewable resources in the making of our books. We make
every effort to use materials that support a sustainable future.

Orca Book Publishers gratefully acknowledges the support
for its publishing programs provided by the following
agencies: the Government of Canada, the Canada Council
for the Arts and the Province of British Columbia through
the BC Arts Council and the Book Publishing Tax Credit.

Artwork created digitally using Corel Painter.
Cover and interior artwork by Cindy Revell

Printed and bound in South Korea.

25 24 23 22 • 1 2 3 4

For all the children in my life—and most especially
for Lauren, Ally & Jack.

—J.R.

For Amanda, the dreamer and thinker, and Connal,
the guy with a can-do attitude.

—C.R.

Nature has given every living thing a way to make a baby.

But where do all those babies come from?

Babies come from their mothers' bodies. When a woman has a baby growing inside of her, she is said to be *pregnant* or *expecting a baby.*

What part of the mother's body does the baby come from?

Under there?

A baby comes from the mother's *womb*, which is just below the stomach. It provides a safe place for the baby to grow.

How does the baby start growing in the first place?

Two ingredients are needed to make a baby. A *sperm* and an *egg*. When the sperm and the egg come together, a baby might begin to grow.

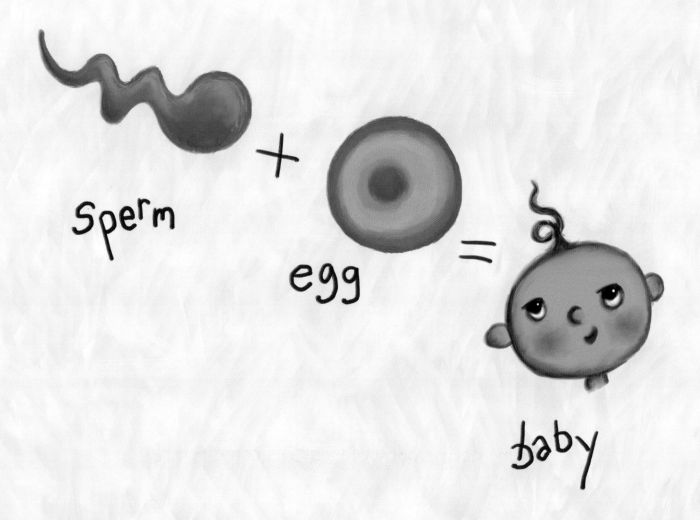

Sperm + egg = baby

Where do the baby ingredients come from?

The sperm comes from the father's body and the egg comes from the mother's body. When it's time to make a baby, these two bodies fit together. The sperm finds the egg, and a seed may be planted in the mother's womb.

That seed starts very little and grows into a big baby.

How does the baby grow?

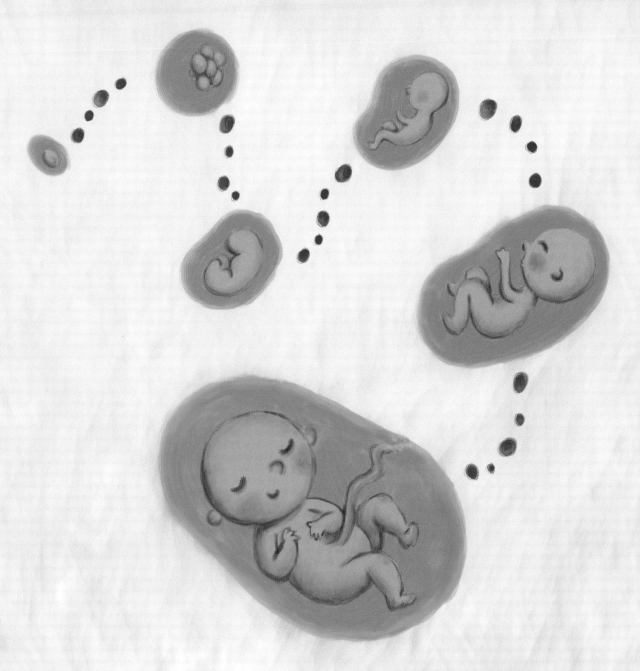

The baby grows when it's fed.

How does the baby eat?

A bit of the mother's food feeds the baby through a special tube called an *umbilical cord*. This connects the baby to its mother.

When the baby is born, the umbilical cord falls off and leaves a belly button.

Look, you have a belly button too!

How long does it take to grow a baby?

Babies usually take nine months to grow. They start out tinier than a pea and can grow to be the size of a watermelon. When the baby is fully developed, it is ready to be born.

month 1

month 2

month 3

month 4

month 5

month 6

month 7

month 8

month 9

How does the baby get out?

When it's time for the baby to be born, he or she is delivered through the mother's birth canal. A baby can be born at home or in a hospital.

Each and every one of us started life as a little seed.

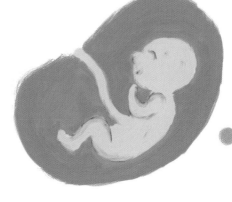

And that little seed became *you!*

Just a Few More Questions

How does the sperm find the egg?

Often when a couple wants to make a baby, the father's penis, which contains the sperm, fits inside the mother's vagina. The sperm then swims through the penis into the vagina, where it will find and fertilize the egg. But babies can be conceived in other ways too. In a process called *in vitro fertilization*, eggs and sperm are combined outside the body. Then fertilized eggs are placed back inside the mother's womb. In either case, a single fertilized egg may be the start of a brand-new baby.

Who helps bring babies into the world?

Many types of doctors and professionals can help with the conception and birth of a new baby. A fertility specialist can help bring the sperm and egg together in the beginning. Midwives are specialists who can assist the mother before, during and after birth. Sometimes a family doctor can help to deliver the baby. If a baby cannot be born through the vagina, or birth canal, an obstetrician can help the baby come out by performing a surgery called a *Cesarean section*. These are just some of the people who can provide support for those expecting a child.

What about babies who were adopted? Where do they come from?

Adopted babies come from a fertilized egg just like every other baby. Sometimes, for many different reasons, a biological mother or birth parent is unable to take care of a new baby. When this happens, the birth parent may give the baby to another family to adopt. The baby then belongs to the adopted family and is loved just as any other baby would be.

What about families with only one mom or dad? Or two moms or two dads? How do different kinds of families have babies?

Babies can be born into all shapes and sizes of families! Sometimes single parents or same-sex parents choose to have a baby on their own or with the help of a doctor. Sometimes they choose to adopt babies. No matter what size or shape a family is, a baby is always loved very, very much.